JUST THE WORD

Avron Levine White

CASA BLANCA |UNITED KINGDOM;
USA; PERU

Copyright © 2017 by
Avron Levine White

All rights reserved. No part of this publication may be reproduced, distributed or transmitted in any form or by any means, without prior written permission.

CASA BLANCA. Dr. Avron Levine White
PO Box 6072
Lake Worth Florida

Avron Levine White -- 1st ed.
ISBN 978-0692945711

Dedicated to my mother Anne
And my wife, Sylvia

Contents

The Pet 1

The Voice 5

The Love 9

The Child 15

The Party 19

The Affair 25

The Argument 31

The Arrangement 37

The Music 41

The Glance 45

The Fcuk 49

The Fight 55

The War 61

The Anchor 65

The Marriage 67

The Separation 73

The Divorce **77**

The Dance **81**

The Tango **85**

The Release **89**

Phone Pals **91**

The Warrioress **97**

True love **101**

Scan QR code to listen to music for this publication

The Pet

Softly Broken

Domestically around

Imperceptibly and gloriously
Housebound
A silent witness who
knows from youth
Sensing danger
Sensing truth
Without judgement
Nor affection turned cold
Your secret life will never be
told
Grieve long and hard which
passed away

Outlive them thrice, quatrille
and a day
Forever more when laid to
rest
A prayer bespoke
For
Who knew you best

The Voice

Show me your voice
And I'll give you the choice
Your preferences understood
With great intonation
and spineless incantation
Come out from under that
Hood!

Is it dancing or singing
Or whingeing with pain
Anesthetic parables
Are perhaps your domain
The droplets of wisdom
pour from your lip
And you suddenly discover

you're really a twit!
Hear me once
Hear me twice
Let me thaw
That block of ice!
Lightening thoughts
Race through your
veins
endless prophecies
futile gains
But somehow
truth rebounds
and stutters:
peripheral platitudes.
And then someone
mutters:

Clear off!.....and let me have some peace

The Love

The love

is

best at the beginning

How the potions of kiss

Clear all actions of blame

All demeanors live by
another name
And how we spoke through
united body
Lying close, we read each
other's eyes
A cryptic interlude brushed
With a smile
The explosion of penetration
Overwhelmed by the heat
And the startling discovery
Of the precious sweet
Lingers like the icing on a
cake

we spoil one another

accepting our groans
the passion, the fashion
the friends we keep –
moan
Our jealously guarded secrets
weep with fear
Within the cocoon of
bareness
We hear others:
speaking, surmising,
wondering if its real
We encrypt, we encode, so
protecting the soul
From the perishing glances of
those who know,
That time is running out.

The years trickle on
But leave us with hope
To get back to before
To system restore
The wonderful balance
Has become a tight rope.
The children despair
And with their convincing stare
They stand in admiration
And confusion

Whilst we display a scaffolding of contradictions
A canopy of restrictions

*Held together by a shoelace
of
Pleasures and pains
Costly recognitions
And difficult gains
The offspring eventually
want to do the same
We hope!*

The Child

The child within you
Creeps around in the past
Reminding you of
Memories surpassed
The final moment

When you gave it up

Those tormenting opponents
When you came unstuck

Well,
the child inside me
screams
and I feel its unjust

But my offspring elated
And ubiquitous enough
Laugh loudly at terror
And football and stuff

My children grew up

In the comfort zone
Penury and disadvantage
Unknown
And when they see other
children in the street
Angry and fighting
For their feet
Deprived, dispossessed, by
parental collapse
Abused, and disused
By circumstantial snap
They, like myself beckon deep
sighs
The inner voice begins to cry
So helpless to right the
Other's wrongs

Relative deprivation
Just becomes a song
Of sixpence and a pocketful
of whys?

The Party

The party is a wishing well

You hope to see the ones to tell

All the darling little secrets

That run through your mind

You hope she drops her
knickers in time.

Well its fair to say
The game is full on
The rules and regulations
Are splattered upon

Ah! The passion of booze
And the intimate news

Jerry had Sally so Sarah had Bill
Regrettably no one was on the pill

But who gives a damn for
DNA detection
The bill still comes from
Child Protection.

Blindness and kindness move
with the drink
And the powders are lined in
a heavenly sync

The mood is compression
With combined ingestion
Now the time is released
From its composite leash
And nothing much is really
said

But the stalking ego is
Well fed
Its all glances and dances
Implied romances
Till the morning light takes a
bite
Of your seemingly
Spinning head

The Affair

Led and wed
Cocooned and landed
Marooned and bandaged
We breed and lead
The newborn.
What your partner doesn't
know is what's left of you

What you don't know
Others do
Stand alone, before an open door
And walk through knowing

You will never return

The bedlock beckons you like a prayer
Tear its fabric if you dare
The underlying secret is there
Compressed in one act of communication

All is revealed in those tender moments

The shoulders rock
The bedclothes drop

The eyes illume at every bloom

Tender lips perform their flirtations
Transmitting to the message destination
Through every bodily pore
the heartbeat is felt
Is it love?
Is it pain?
Is it someone else's gain
The rocking horse splits your life in two
Part becomes habit
And part of it is you

The world de-constructs
Throughout this passion
And leaves you stranded
In unknown fashion

Be true to yourself
And define the mind

Begin your time again.

The Argument

**Pin the tail on the donkey
Smack this ass and let it run**

You're really having loads of fun

And though riddled with untold delight

This is an argument
not a fight!
I disagree with your enchantment
Let go of this fear
That drives the soul
Forgive the trespass
That blazed your story
And enter claims that truly hold.

*Never before has "word"
mattered so much
Intrepid thoughts with the
power of touch
You spoke harshly and with
venomous truth
And were answered with lies
uncouth
Consider please
This other option
To nail the point
with complete adoption
Let go of the position and
down the size
There may be room for
Compromise*

Dismantle your passion for being right
When practical matters vary ever so slight
Yield a few yards and position hold
The matter is granted but remains untold
All is fair with chit and chat
A clever dare is mostly that
However
When you achieve your Final goal
You must be sensitive as to how its told

The Arrangement

They are living like sister and brother
He has his mistress and she has her lover
Once, when formerly wed

They slipped into bed
Endlessly,
But how the ravages of
Time
Cease to confine
And gradually unwind
The entanglements of
children and jobs
The impossible sobs
The conflicting aspirations
Of several generations
Unhinged with regret
every wrong step

The Music

Enter the bland wagon
The rapturous horn blown
Foot stomping blares
A single voice soars

And escapes in mid air
How many times have we
listened to the rap
And thought
This is a "slap"
The incomprehensible lyric
And effervescing spirit
Mystifies anger and torment

Now we are listening to the
culture of minds
The language of deprivation
The words of the unkind
We feel the pressure of the
unfulfilled quest
The dangers of innovation

The tricks of the test

Hark back to days when melody ruled
The hook was clear and the mood was "cool"
Love is glad, then its bad,
And then
Its better again.
So What!, Said Miles.
But now we are confronted
With the unwanted
And it is clear to all where we are going wrong...
The sweetness of life isn't in the song

Its in the words that cry for help...
The ones that demolish the unjust self
Will it leave us with a hope?

The Glance

Expressly hidden in mid-face
Abstractly risen
In the nick of time
Unstudied, unforced
Quick witted and blind
The glance compares

Your perception to mine
Was it the body language?
Or the soup?
Which spilled across the table
In one fell swoop.
Whilst in mid-word
Of consequential proportion
The expressed intent
Was now distortion
The rest of us laughed
Except for one
Save for the sound
Of a wiping cloth

The glance betrays
The inner voice

Unfiltered, unhushed
To any choice
Covertly
And
Unbearably loud,
Forever viewed amongst the crowd
The glance gives snapshot
At shutter speed
the true intent behind the deed!

The Fcuk

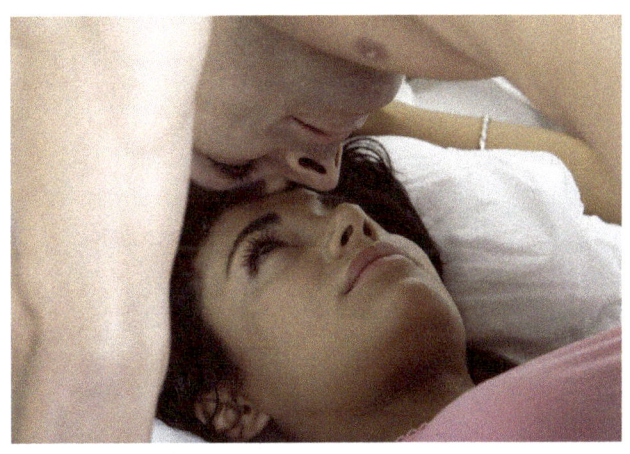

Caw! Scattered clothes on the floor
What's there you've never seen before
A quiet undress
A slow caress

The collapse of inhibition
The physical erudition
Slow long undulating licks
The helmet pops, reveals its slit
The bianco forest and impassioned clit
Is ringed and shaven
An easy grip
The body explores
And opens doors
Pulsating contractions
Creates reactions
Her tongue rings round the lingering tip
In full manness

They connect the hips
And in slow gentle motion
Like winding clock
Full penetrations of aching cock

Withheld, enjoyed and not too fast
The beat of passion is out at last
The hands explore
And touch adores
The gentle nipple twist

Brushing over legs and feet
The hands like leaves

Whisper the seat
The occasional prod
Throw out the heat
With changed position
He can view the feet
Her head below from backshot timbre
Clutching pillow
And holding limber
A quicker pace, now fluid entry
A g spot moan says not too gently
Encouraged by the stroking hair
And visions of such derriere

The matter overturns
And she on top
Gently caresses the two-ball top
The body tenses
The rhythm holds
They close each other's bodies bold
She leans forward for tongue in kiss
An impassioned thrust
Creates the bliss
One final burst of frenzied friction
To slower moves and now conviction

*The body and heart soften to the glance
And warm embrace
Confirms this chance,*

*Unbonded,
Unhinged,
Unfed by emotion,
Nevertheless
Gratitude,
And some devotion*

.

The Fight

Embattled species
Indefinite destitution
Hang on m......f......r
There is a solution

Go to town on the witch
Mixing tongue with dilution
The vivacious cometh
With angry diminution

And when that is
All through
You have
The shrew
Antennae unfold
Like an Eagle on the go
A mini disc of sounds
And expired grounds
Now big sister
There's no place to hide
The predator took away

Your pride

Parade your conscience
Display your thighs
Clench your fists
And go for the eyes
She landed one upon his chin
He ducked and lunged
She kneed him in

He fell to the floor with an
agonising squeal
And grabbed the knife
Just by his heel
He lifted high
the blade of threat

Which she grabbed
And plunged deep in his chest
She looked aghast,
in disbelief
and stillness spoke with some relief
But then the staggering movements come
The fluid spills wild,
The passion done

What a relief
The time is up
The alarm clock rang

And she rolled over on to soft satin sheets of gold

The War

Panic in the heart
As you enter dizzy spin
No one will notice
The state that you are in

From the fractured sins

To the fires of damnation
Lay your hands on earth's
Shattered vibrations

Give over to the words
They speak for the youth
Actions defy gravity
But only in truth

We wait for the message
Its nearly complete
Flesh tingles with excitement
As you land on your feet

Lord knows how you missed
The speeding bullet passed

Tearing innocent flesh
Leaving its horrific gash
And..Suddenly
The body grows old
And gone is the pink
Whilst a hero for minutes
Swept away in a blink

Praise nigh the speechless
deities
And their spokesman's
judgements bold

The angry politicians
The incompetence told

We blame each other
We blame the gods
We blame the oil
We blame the sods
Why are we fighting
With such human blindness
When all that is required
Is human mindness

It's the complex gift of understanding
And sympathetic deeds
Without demanding
Anything….in return

The Anchor

Never moving from its perch
It sees all
Hears all
And feels the dirt

The Marriage

Marriage can be
a bed of lies
First its love
But when it dies
What is left is compromise?

What would you expect from
such almighty thunder
Break the rules and you go
under

The pain, the strain,
tells you….only once
That this selfless love
which inspired the union
Was an endorphin fueled
Amorphic intrusion

Hopeless and helpless
judgement is clouded
Then we are torn and
hopelessly shrouded

But we needed that
in the earlier years
To stabilize our worst fears
Never knowing whose child
it is
The lineage, inheritance and
all that biz
But now
A judgmental view is looming
The parameters of which
seem somewhat dooming
A furtive glance, the wrong
dance
Someone gives you a chance

To express yourself as an individual
And quickly you slam on the brakes

Undermined is the secret self
So to adopt a strategy of stealth
Uncertainty and loss
Dare you risk the dross?
The unspeakable recognition
of an emotional gunpoint
And lo and behold, the verbal blast
implodes
With unexpected precision

The words enter
Your heart
mushrooming like a cloud
Slowly, painfully and almost
imperceptibly
tearing the love into anger
And the anger into despair

The bonding becomes
Bondage

We try to get out
But the loosening knot is
never felt
All we want is a little more
room

The Separation

Lying in wait

Prostate
And in the mind
There is a culpable partner
struggling
To heal the wounds
Of another time
A new life grows
Bold and untold
Breaking with constriction
And felling contradiction
You point in new directions
Whilst old habits and
inhibition
Slowly die
Gone are some memories
Consigned to fading canvas

A once life is
now in dusty closed abyss

Conceived
Now bereaved
A slow process of
Changing from
What you perceived
To what you can see

We wept and danced
Saying goodbye to sorrow
He may keep his throne
But she keeps the drones

The friends and relations

Whose tender deliberations
Part company

Assets divided and children
decided
Like a poker players hand
The hearts and diamonds
Live in separate suits.

The Divorce

I left my husband
I left my wife
Been living on the edge of a knife
The anger left barren
The story untold
Is everyone healthy?
Is everyone old?

The children grew through
our daily routines
Wild promises made
To give them their dreams

Now left with solitude
And a manner of peace
Tormenting silence raging
Like the surf on a reef
We cannot give back, The
messages and the
Lies
The bewilderment
Which killed the sinuous ties
Now all is barren
All is cold

The Dance

Widely turned
And narrowly expressed
Footwork and tension
Has made the rest

Waltz or tango
Across the floor
Salsa, merengue
A little more

Her hair thrown back
Across the shoulder
Make his steps a little bolder
Heaven forbid the dangerous flirt
As the eyes fall just below the skirt
The woman can see determination
A power spin sends expectation

Positioned well
They cast their spell
Upon one another
The axis of balance
Holds their moves
And a centrifugal movement
Bonds them
Like a bandoneon.

The Tango

Bosom to bosom
Head to head
Adornments and firuletes
From the leg

The curved delights
Of embellished lace
Impale upon us
To full embrace

The twists, the turns
The scattered steps
Lead two strangers
In united depths
Of controlled emotion
And passionate devotion
To a prayer of movement......

Dance me to the music
Of the tandas

So forlorn
Bring me to the perfect end
of every single song
Celebrate the knowing
Of this total stranger
Gone

The Release

A tantalizing buffet
of Eros fueled display
Came to mind in unexpected rushes
Like a magnet of truth
Every effort to postpone

The endemic failed
They cleared their desks
and were conspicuous by
their absence
Where have they gone, one
asked?

"To meditate."

Phone Pals

Cookies aren't so sweet anymore!

Alone with the universe in
private spore
Earplugged and yielding

Unwilling eyes
An impenetrable visage
Won't recognize
No longer available
For a compassionate glance
We walk alone by chance
amongst millions,
All of whom
talking, thinking, feeling and
connecting with the moon
anyone….
Except….
The person
Next to us
Close to us

Raise high your instrument
Of dogmatic verse!
The pictures and videos
What are they worth?
A lifetime of fragmented
moments?

We document,
We record,
Our experience in time

We share:
with those who can't be with us
We share with those who
don't want to be with us

We share with those who just
wish we weren't there
Ahh!
What the eye doesn't see the
heart doesn't grieve
We cease to see who is in
front of us
To understand the song of
their conversation.
Have we stolen the voice?
Are our hearts and souls
In the cloud!
My WhatsApp.
Your Viber.

What the Skype are we
talking about!
And someone,
A Stranger
Will be watching us,
recording us, and feeding us
Cookies!

The Warrioress

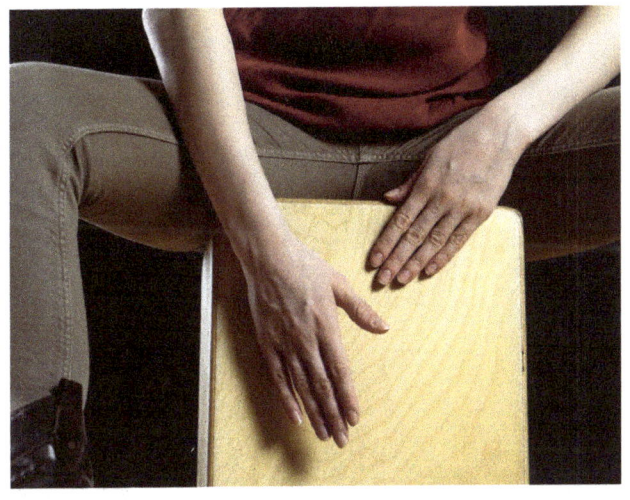

Sitting streetwise
Alone
On her cajon
Whilst midnight urban crews
Steamroll their
SUV'S in a stir fry of

R&B and hip hop funk
She is laying down
Finger rolling,
Fruity,
Funk
Slapping it large
On the edge of the box
Urban proud,
She sits tight
and strong
Across the wood

The large antique gold
Bohemian cross with
Black macramé strap
Glistens in the streetlight

A crowd gathers and
A few start to dance
And the pace gathers
Suddenly this wild one
Picks her up off the cajon
And pushes her up against
the stone wall

Screaming loud
"you don't mess with me!"
She brought her knee
At cannonball speed
into crotch
And this predator
Went down like

A sack of seed
The police sirens
blasted up the street
She grabbed her cajon
By the hole at the back
And ran like lightening
Into darkness
The crowd dispersed
With a slow walk
In different directions
Leaving the
Agonized one...On the ground

True love

The true love
Is found
Through a maze of
Imperfect perception
An imponderable
incompleteness

That somehow
Yields a certain faith in truth
From broken promises
We heal
To newborn thoughts
Of unprotected imagination
We dwell on the connection
Like a bridge to the soul
We have each other
Before we grow old

Most of what we say
Comes from the face without words

Although
Words
Do surprise us
Like poetry or verse

There is power
That binds our connection
From the universe of light
We accept the reception

Now that nothing but the
truth is told
All is forgiven
No matter how old
It matters not
whatever

Misdeed
That somehow held us
We have now been freed

www.ingramcontent.com/pod-product-compliance
Lightning Source LLC
Chambersburg PA
CBHW062112290426
44110CB00023B/2789